SHADES OF Grey

I0896134

FOR HOME ACCENTS AND TRENDY FASHIONS

that look good anywhere and everywhere, choose from these 11 handsome designs to crochet in neutral greys. To demonstrate their versatility, some are also shown in alternate colors.

LEISURE ARTS, INC. • Maumelle, Arkansas

Cabled Afghan

●●○○ **EASY** **Finished Size:** Approximately 48" x 65" (124.5 cm x 165 cm)

SHOPPING LIST

Yarn (Jumbo Weight) 7

[5.29 ounces, 46 yards

(150 grams, 42 meters) per skein]:

☐ 20 skeins

Crochet Hook

☐ Size Q (15 mm)

or size needed for gauge

GAUGE INFORMATION

In pattern,

7 hdc and 5 rows = 6" (15.25 cm)

Gauge Swatch: 6" (15.25 cm) square

Ch 8.

Work same as Afghan for 5 rows: 7 hdc.

Finish off.

Each row is worked across length of Afghan.

AFGHAN

Ch 77, place marker in second ch from hook for st placement.

Row 1 (Right side)**:** Hdc in second ch from hook and in each ch across: 76 hdc.

Note: Loop a short piece of yarn around any stitch to mark Row 1 as **right** side.

Row 2: Ch 1, turn; working in horizontal bar of each hdc ***(Fig. A)***, hdc in first hdc and each hdc across.

Fig. A

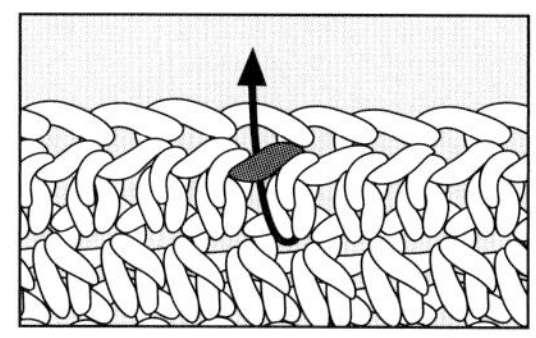

Repeat Row 2 for pattern until Afghan measures approximately 47" (119.5 cm) from beginning ch, ending by working a **wrong** side row.

Edging: Ch 1, turn; working in horizontal bar of sts across last row, 2 sc in first hdc, sc in each hdc across to last hdc, 2 sc in last hdc; working in ends of rows, sc evenly across; working in free loops of beginning ch ***(Fig. 1, page 30)***; 2 sc in first ch, sc in each ch across to marked ch, 2 sc in marked ch, remove marker; working in ends of rows, sc evenly across; join with slip st to first sc, finish off.

Design by Terry Kimbrough.

Ripple Afghan

●●○○ **EASY** **Finished Size:** Approximately 49" x 65" (124.5 cm x 165 cm)

SHOPPING LIST

Yarn (Medium Weight) MEDIUM 4

[5 ounces, 250 yards

(141.7 grams, 228 meters) per skein]:

- ☐ Dk Grey - 5 skeins
- ☐ Lt Grey - 5 skeins

[6 ounces, 315 yards

(170.1 grams, 288 meters) per skein]:

- ☐ Yellow - 1 skein

Crochet Hook

- ☐ Size H (5 mm)
  or size needed for gauge

GAUGE INFORMATION

In pattern, one repeat (one ch-1 sp and 12 dc) = 3¼" (8.25 cm); 9 rows = 5" (12.75 cm)

Gauge Swatch: 6¾"w x 5"h (17.25 cm x 12.75 cm)

With Dk Grey, ch 30.

Work same as Rows 1-9; at end of Row 9, do **not** change colors, finish off: 26 dc and 2 ch-1 sps.

AFGHAN

With Dk Grey, ch 199.

Row 1: Dc in fifth ch from hook and in next 4 chs **(4 skipped chs count as first dc plus 1 skipped ch)**, (dc, ch 1, dc) in next ch, dc in next 5 chs, ★ skip next 2 chs, dc in next 5 chs, (dc, ch 1, dc) in next ch, dc in next 5 chs; repeat from ★ across to last 2 chs, skip next ch, dc in last ch: 182 dc and 15 ch-1 sps.

Rows 2 and 3: Ch 3 **(counts as first dc)**, turn; skip next dc, dc in next 5 dc, (dc, ch 1, dc) in next ch-1 sp, dc in next 5 dc, ★ skip next 2 dc, dc in next 5 dc, (dc, ch 1, dc) in next ch-1 sp, dc in next 5 dc; repeat from ★ across to last 2 dc, skip next dc, dc in last dc.

Row 4: Repeat Row 2 changing to Yellow in last dc *(Fig. 5, page 31)*; cut Dk Grey.

Row 5: Repeat Row 2 changing to Dk Grey in last dc; cut Yellow.

Rows 6-8: Repeat Row 2, 3 times.

Row 9: Repeat Row 2 changing to Lt Grey in last dc; cut Dk Grey.

Stripe Sequence: ★ 4 Rows Lt Grey, 1 row Yellow, 4 rows Lt Grey, 4 rows Dk Grey, 1 row Yellow, 4 rows Dk Grey; repeat from ★ for sequence.

Working in Stripe Sequence, repeat Row 2 for pattern until Afghan measures approximately 65" (165 cm) from lowest point on ripple to highest point on last row, ending by working a complete Stripe Sequence.

Finish off.

Rug

●●○○ EASY **Finished Size:** 35½" (90 cm) diameter

SHOPPING LIST

Yarn (Bulky Weight) BULKY 5

[3.5 ounces, 95 yards

(100 grams, 86 meters) per skein]:

☐ 6 skeins

Crochet Hook

☐ Size M/N (9 mm)

or size needed for gauge

GAUGE INFORMATION

Rnds 1-4 = 7" (17.75 cm) diameter

RUG

Ch 7; join with slip st to form a ring.

Rnd 1 (Right side)**:** Ch 5 **(counts as first dc plus ch 2, now and throughout)**, (dc in ring, ch 2) 13 times; join with slip st to first dc: 14 dc and 14 ch-2 sps.

Note: Loop a short piece of yarn around any stitch to mark Rnd 1 as **right** side.

Rnd 2: Ch 3 **(counts as first dc, now and throughout)**, 2 dc in next ch-2 sp, (dc in next dc, 2 dc in next ch-2 sp) around; join with slip st to first dc: 42 dc.

Rnd 3: Ch 1, sc in sp **before** joining ***(Fig. 6, page 31)***, ★ ch 3, skip next 3 dc, sc in sp **before** next dc; repeat from ★ around to last 3 dc, ch 1, skip last 3 dc, hdc in first sc to form last ch-3 sp: 14 ch-3 sps.

Rnd 4: Ch 1, 2 sc in last ch-3 sp made, (ch 3, 2 sc in next ch-3 sp) around, ch 1, hdc in first sc to form last ch-3 sp.

Rnd 5: Ch 5, dc in last ch-3 sp made, ch 2, (dc, ch 2) twice in next ch-3 sp and in each ch-3 sp around; join with slip st to first dc: 28 ch-2 sps.

Rnd 6: Slip st in next ch-2 sp, ch 6 **(counts as first dc plus ch 3, now and throughout)**, (dc in next ch-2 sp, ch 3) around; join with slip st to first dc.

Rnd 7: (Slip st, ch 3, 3 dc) in next ch-3 sp, 4 dc in next ch-3 sp and in each ch-3 sp around; join with slip st to first dc: 112 dc.

Rnd 8: Ch 1, sc in sp **before** joining, ch 7, skip next 4 dc, ★ sc in sp **before** next dc, ch 7, skip next 4 dc; repeat from ★ around; join with slip st to first sc: 28 ch-7 sps.

Rnd 9: (Slip st, ch 3, 8 dc) in next ch-7 sp, sc in next ch-7 sp, ★ 9 dc in next ch-7 sp, sc in next ch-7 sp; repeat from ★ around; join with slip st to first dc: 140 sts.

Rnd 10: Ch 1, sc in same st as joining, (ch 4, skip next 3 dc, sc in next dc) twice, ★ ch 4, skip next sc, sc in next dc, (ch 4, skip next 3 dc, sc in next dc) twice; repeat from ★ around to last sc, ch 1, skip last sc, dc in first sc to form last ch-4 sp: 42 ch-4 sps.

Rnd 11: Ch 5, dc in last ch-4 sp made, ch 2, (dc, ch 2) twice in next ch-4 sp and in each ch-4 sp around; join with slip st to first dc: 84 ch-2 sps.

Rnd 12: Slip st in next ch-2 sp, ch 6, skip next ch-2 sp, dc in next ch-2 sp, ★ ch 3, skip next ch-2 sp, dc in next ch-2 sp; repeat from ★ around to last ch-2 sp, ch 1, skip last ch-2 sp, hdc in first dc to form last ch-3 sp: 42 ch-3 sps.

Rnd 13: Ch 3, dc in last ch-3 sp made, ch 1, ★ (2 dc, ch 2, 2 dc) in next ch-3 sp, ch 1; repeat from ★ around, 2 dc in same sp as first dc, ch 1, sc in first dc to form last ch-2 sp: 84 sps.

Rnd 14: Ch 3, dc in last ch-2 sp made, sc in next ch-1 sp, ★ (2 dc, ch 2, 2 dc) in next ch-2 sp, sc in next ch-1 sp; repeat from ★ around, 2 dc in same sp as first dc, ch 1, sc in first dc to form last ch-2 sp: 42 ch-2 sps.

Rnd 15: Ch 3, dc in last ch-2 sp made, ch 1, (2 dc, ch 1) twice in next ch-2 sp and in each ch-2 sp around, 2 dc in same sp as first dc, sc in first dc to form last ch-1 sp: 84 ch-1 sps.

Rnd 16: Ch 3, dc in last ch-1 sp made, sc in next ch-1 sp, ★ (2 dc, ch 2, 2 dc) in next ch-1 sp, sc in next ch-1 sp; repeat from ★ around, 2 dc in same sp as first dc, ch 1, sc in first dc to form last ch-2 sp: 42 ch-2 sps.

Rnd 17: Ch 3, dc in last ch-2 sp made, ch 1, ★ (2 dc, ch 2, 2 dc) in next ch-2 sp, ch 1; repeat from ★ around, 2 dc in same sp as first dc, ch 1, sc in first dc to form last ch-2 sp: 84 sps.

Rnd 18: Ch 3, dc in last ch-2 sp made, sc in next ch-1 sp, ★ (2 dc, ch 2, 2 dc) in next ch-2 sp, sc in next ch-1 sp; repeat from ★ around, 2 dc in same sp as first dc, ch 1, sc in first dc to form last ch-2 sp: 42 ch-2 sps.

Rnd 19: Ch 3, dc in last ch-2 sp made, ch 2, (2 dc, ch 2) twice in next ch-2 sp and in each ch-2 sp around, 2 dc in same sp as first dc, ch 1, sc in first dc to form last ch-2 sp: 84 ch-2 sps.

Rnd 20: Ch 3, dc in last ch-2 sp made, ch 1, sc in next ch-2 sp, ch 1, ★ (2 dc, ch 2, 2 dc) in next ch-2 sp, ch 1, sc in next ch-2 sp, ch 1; repeat from ★ around, 2 dc in same sp as first dc, ch 1, sc in first dc to form last ch-2 sp: 210 sts and 126 sps.

Rnd 21: Ch 1, sc in last ch-2 sp made and in next 2 dc and next ch-1 sp, skip next sc, sc in next ch-1 sp and in next 2 dc, ★ (sc, ch 3, sc) in next ch-2 sp, sc in next 2 dc and in next ch-1 sp, skip next sc, sc in next ch-1 sp and in next 2 dc; repeat from ★ around, sc in same sp as first sc, ch 3; join with slip st to first sc, finish off.

Design by Sue Galucki.

Plush Pillow

Shown on page 10.

EASY **Finished Size:** 18½" wide x 16" high (47 cm x 40.5 cm)

SHOPPING LIST

Yarn (Medium Weight) MEDIUM 4
[4 ounces, 212 yards
(113 grams, 194 meters) per skein]:
- ☐ 4 skeins

Crochet Hook
- ☐ Size I (5.5 mm)
  or size needed for gauge

Additional Supplies
- ☐ 18½" x 16" (47 cm x 40.5 cm) pillow form **or** 20" x 33" (51 cm x 84 cm) fabric and polyester fiberfill
- ☐ Yarn needle

GAUGE INFORMATION

In Crocodile Stitch, 3 Scales and 10 rows = 4" (10 cm)
In Back pattern, 11 dc and 7 rows = 3½" (9 cm)
Gauge Swatch: 3½" (9 cm) square
Ch 13.
Row 1: Dc in fourth ch from hook **(3 skipped chs count as first dc)** and in each ch across: 11 dc.
Rows 2-7: Ch 3 **(counts as first dc)**, turn; dc in next dc and in each dc across.
Finish off.

FRONT

Ch 82.

Row 1 (Foundation row - Wrong side row)**:** Dc in fourth ch from hook **(3 skipped chs count as first dc)**, ★ ch 1, skip next 2 chs, dc in next ch, ch 1, skip next 2 chs, 2 dc in next ch; repeat from ★ across: 14 2-dc groups, 13 dc, and 26 chs.

Row 2 (Scale row)**:** Ch 1, work 5 dc down post of last dc made working over beginning end ***(Fig. A)***, ch 1, rotate Foundation Row and work 5 dc up post of next dc to form a Scale ***(Figs. B & C)***, ★ skip next ch, slip st in next dc, skip next ch, work 5 dc down post of next dc, ch 1, rotate piece and work 5 dc up post of next dc; repeat from ★ across, slip st around post of same dc: 14 Scales.

Fig. A

Fig. B

Fig. C

Row 3 (Foundation row)**:** Ch 4 **(counts as first dc plus ch 1, now and throughout)**, 2 dc in next slip st (between Scales) ***(Fig. D)***, ch 1, dc in center of next Scale ***(Fig. E)***, ★ ch 1, 2 dc in next slip st, ch 1, dc in center of next Scale; repeat from ★ across: 13 2-dc groups, 14 dc, and 26 chs.

Fig. D

Fig. E

Row 4 (Scale row)**:** Turn; slip st in first dc, ★ skip next ch, work 5 dc down post of next dc, ch 1, rotate piece and work 5 dc up post of next dc, skip next ch, slip st in next dc; repeat from ★ across: 13 Scales.

Row 5 (Foundation row)**:** Ch 3 **(counts as first dc, now and throughout)**, turn; dc in first slip st, ★ ch 1, dc in center of next Scale, ch 1, 2 dc in next slip st; repeat from ★ across: 14 2-dc groups, 13 dc, and 26 chs.

Row 6 (Scale row)**:** Ch 1, work 5 dc down post of last dc made, ch 1, rotate piece and work 5 dc up post of next dc to form a Scale, ★ skip next ch, slip st in next dc, skip next ch, work 5 dc down post of next dc, ch 1, rotate piece and work 5 dc up post of next dc; repeat from ★ across, slip st around post of same dc: 14 Scales.

Repeat Rows 3-6 for pattern until Front measures approximately 16" (40.5 cm) from beginning ch, ending by working Row 6; do **not** finish off.

BACK

Row 1: Ch 1, turn; 3 sc in center of first Scale, 3 sc in next slip st, 2 sc in center of next Scale, (2 sc in next slip st, 2 sc in center of next Scale) across to last slip st, 3 sc in last slip st, 3 sc in center of last Scale: 58 sc.

Row 2: Ch 3, turn; dc in next st and in each st across.

Repeat Row 2 until Back measures same as Front; finish off.

If desired, using piece as a guide, make a pillow form or cover a purchased pillow form.

With **wrong** side together, whipstitch across 2 sides ***(Figs. 7a & b, page 31)***; insert pillow form and whipstitch across remaining side.

Design by Lisa Gentry.

Cup Cozy

EASY **Finished Size:** 2¾" high x 9¾" long (7 cm x 25 cm)

SHOPPING LIST

Yarn (Medium Weight) 4 MEDIUM

- ☐ 35 yards (32 meters)

Crochet Hook

- ☐ Size G (4 mm) **or** size needed for gauge

Additional Supplies

- ☐ Yarn needle
- ☐ Sewing needle and thread
- ☐ 5/8" (16 mm) buttons - 3

GAUGE INFORMATION

In pattern,

8 sc and 10 rows = 2" (5 cm)

Gauge Swatch: 2" (5 cm) square

Ch 9.

Row 1: Sc in second ch from hook and in each ch across: 8 sc.

Rows 2-10: Ch 1, turn; working in Back Loops Only ***(Fig. 2, page 30)***, sc in each sc across.

Finish off.

COZY

Ch 40.

Row 1: Sc in second ch from hook and in each ch across: 39 sc.

Cozy is worked in Back Loops Only throughout ***(Fig. 2, page 30)***.

Row 2 (Right side)**:** Ch 1, turn; sc in each sc across.

Note: Loop a short piece of yarn around any stitch to mark Row 2 as **right** side.

Row 3 (Buttonhole row)**:** Ch 1, turn; sc in first 2 sc, ch 2, skip next 2 sc, sc in next sc and in each sc across: 37 sc and one ch-2 sp.

Row 4: Ch 1, turn; sc in each sc and in each ch across: 39 sc.

Rows 5 and 6: Ch 1, turn; sc in each sc across.

Rows 7-14: Repeat Rows 3-6 twice.

Finish off.

Design by Michele Wilcox.

Zigzag Dishcloth

●●○○ EASY **Finished Size:** Approximately 13½" (34.5 cm) square

SHOPPING LIST

Yarn (Medium Weight) MEDIUM 4

[2.1 ounces, 105 yards

(60 grams, 96 meters) per skein]:

☐ Grey - 2 skeins

[2.8 ounces, 140 yards

(80 grams, 128 meters) per skein]:

☐ White - 50 yards (45.5 meters)

Crochet Hook

☐ Size H (5 mm)

or size needed for gauge

GAUGE INFORMATION

In pattern,

(work Cluster, sc) twice = 3" (7.5 cm)

STITCH GUIDE

CLUSTER (uses next 5 sts)

★ YO, insert hook in **next** st, YO and pull up a loop, YO and draw through 2 loops on hook; repeat from ★ 4 times **more**, YO and draw through all 6 loops on hook.

INSTRUCTIONS

With Grey, ch 50.

Row 1 (Right side)**:** Sc in second ch from hook, ★ skip next 2 chs, 5 dc in next ch, skip next 2 chs, sc in next ch; repeat from ★ across: 8 5-dc groups.

Note: Loop a short piece of yarn around any stitch to mark Row 1 as **right** side.

Row 2: Ch 2, turn; (YO, insert hook in **next** dc, YO and pull up a loop, YO and draw through 2 loops on hook) twice, YO and draw through all 3 loops on hook, ch 2, sc in next dc, ch 2, (work Cluster, ch 2, sc in next dc, ch 2) across to last 3 sts, (YO, insert hook in **next** st, YO and pull up a loop, YO and draw through 2 loops on hook) 3 times, YO and draw through all 4 loops on hook: 7 Clusters.

Row 3: Ch 1, turn; sc in first st, ★ 5 dc in next sc, skip next 2 chs, sc in next st; repeat from ★ across; finish off: 8 5-dc groups.

Row 4: With **wrong** side facing, join White with slip st in first sc; ch 2, (YO, insert hook in **next** dc, YO and pull up a loop, YO and draw through 2 loops on hook) twice, YO and draw through all 3 loops on hook, ch 2, sc in next dc, ch 2, (work Cluster, ch 2, sc in next dc, ch 2) across to last 3 sts, (YO, insert hook in **next** st, YO and pull up a loop, YO and draw through 2 loops on hook) 3 times, YO and draw through all 4 loops on hook: 7 Clusters.

Row 5: Ch 1, turn; sc in first st, ★ 5 dc in next sc, skip next 2 chs, sc in next st; repeat from ★ across; finish off: 8 5-dc groups.

Row 6: With Grey, repeat Row 4: 7 Clusters.

Row 7: Ch 1, turn; sc in first st, ★ 5 dc in next sc, skip next 2 chs, sc in next st; repeat from ★ across: 8 5-dc groups.

Row 8: Ch 2, turn; (YO insert hook in **next** dc, YO and pull up a loop, YO and draw through 2 loops on hook) twice, YO and draw through all 3 loops on hook, ch 2, sc in next dc, ch 2, (work Cluster, ch 2, sc in next dc, ch 2) across to last 3 sts, (YO, insert hook in **next** st, YO and pull up a loop, YO and draw through 2 loops on hook) 3 times, YO and draw through all 4 loops on hook: 7 Clusters.

Rows 9-19: Repeat Rows 7 and 8, 5 times; then repeat Row 7 once **more**; at end of Row 19, finish off.

Rows 20-24: Repeat Rows 4-8; at end of Row 24, finish off: 7 Clusters.

Edging: With **right** side facing, join White with sc in first st ***(see Joining With Sc, page 30)***; sc evenly around entire dishcloth, working 3 sc in each corner; join with slip st to first sc, finish off.

Design by Rhona Czepiel.

Trendsetter Hat

Shown on page 18.

●●○○ EASY **Fits Head Circumference:** 20-22" (51-56 cm)

SHOPPING LIST

Yarn (Medium Weight) MEDIUM 4

[3.5 ounces, 170 yards (100 grams, 156 meters) per skein]:

- ☐ Grey - 1 skein
- ☐ Red - 1 skein

Crochet Hook

- ☐ Size J (6 mm) **or** size needed for gauge

Additional Supplies

- ☐ Split-ring marker **or** scrap yarn
- ☐ Yarn needle

GAUGE INFORMATION

13 sc and 15 rows/rnds = 4" (10 cm)

Gauge Swatch: 4" (10 cm) square

Ch 14.

Row 1: Sc in second ch from hook and in each ch across: 13 sc.

Rows 2-15: Ch 1, turn; sc in each sc across.

Finish off.

STITCH GUIDE

SINGLE CROCHET 2 TOGETHER ***(abbreviated sc2tog)***

Pull up a loop in each of next 2 sc, YO and draw through all 3 loops on hook (**counts as one sc**).

BAND

With Red and leaving a long end for sewing, ch 16.

Row 1 (Right side)**:** Sc in second ch from hook and in next 6 chs, 3 sc in next ch, sc in last 7 chs: 17 sc.

Note: Loop a short piece of yarn around any stitch to mark Row 1 as **right** side.

Row 2: Ch 1, turn; sc in first sc, skip next sc, sc in next 6 sc, 3 sc in next sc, sc in next 6 sc, skip next sc, sc in last sc; finish off.

Row 3: With **right** side facing, join Grey with sc in first sc *(see Joining With Sc, page 30)*; skip next sc, sc in next 6 sc, 3 sc in next sc, sc in next 6 sc, skip next sc, sc in last sc.

Row 4: Ch 1, turn; sc in first sc, skip next sc, sc in next 6 sc, 3 sc in next sc, sc in next 6 sc, skip next sc, sc in last sc; finish off.

Row 5: With **right** side facing, join Red with sc in first sc; skip next sc, sc in next 6 sc, 3 sc in next sc, sc in next 6 sc, skip next sc, sc in last sc.

Row 6: Ch 1, turn; sc in first sc, skip next sc, sc in next 6 sc, 3 sc in next sc, sc in next 6 sc, skip next sc, sc in last sc; finish off.

Row 7: With **right** side facing, join Grey with sc in first sc; skip next sc, sc in next 6 sc, 3 sc in next sc, sc in next 6 sc, skip next sc, sc in last sc.

Rows 8-19: Repeat Rows 4-7, 3 times.

Rows 20-68: Ch 1, turn; sc in first sc, skip next sc, sc in next 6 sc, 3 sc in next sc, sc in next 6 sc, skip next sc, sc in last sc.

Finish off leaving a long end for sewing.

Place marker in first sc on Row 50 to mark Body placement.

Overlap **right** side of last 4 rows with **wrong** side of first 4 rows, forming a tube. Using long end from beginning ch, sew piece together. With long end from Row 68, sew last row in place on **wrong** side.

BODY

Rnd 1: With **right** side facing, join Grey with sc in end of marked row; working in end of rows and through **both** thicknesses where Band overlaps, sc in each row around; join with slip st to first sc: 64 sc.

Rnd 2: Ch 1, sc in same st as joining and in each sc around; do **not** join, place marker to mark beginning of rnd ***(see Markers, page 29)***.

Rnds 3-15: Sc in each sc around.

Rnd 16: (Sc in next 6 sc, sc2tog) around: 56 sc.

Rnd 17: (Sc in next 5 sc, sc2tog) around: 48 sc.

Rnd 18: (Sc in next 4 sc, sc2tog) around: 40 sc.

Rnd 19: (Sc in next 3 sc, sc2tog) around: 32 sc.

Rnd 20: (Sc in next 2 sc, sc2tog) around: 24 sc.

Rnd 21: (Sc in next sc, sc2tog) around: 16 sc.

Rnd 22: Sc2tog around; slip st in next sc, finish off leaving a long end for sewing: 8 sc.

Thread yarn needle with long end and weave needle through sts on Rnd 22 ***(Fig. A)***; gather **tightly** and secure end.

Fig. A

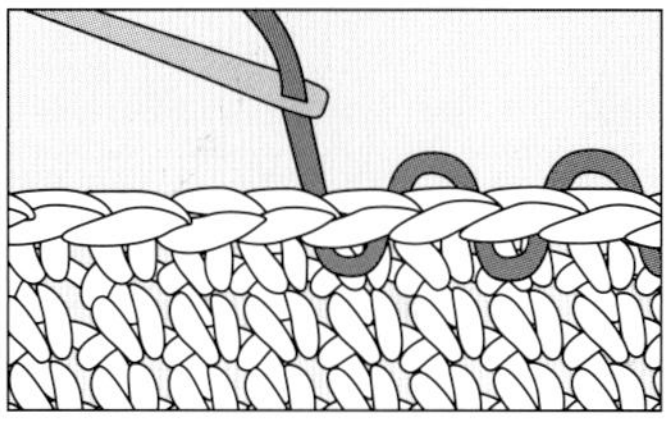

Design by Kristi Simpson.

Sexton Braid Hat & Scarf

●●○○ **EASY**

• • • • **Finished Sizes: Hat** - Fits 20" (51 cm) head circumference; **Scarf** - 9" wide x 54" long (23 cm x 137 cm) • • • • •

SHOPPING LIST

Yarn (Medium Weight) 4 MEDIUM

[4 ounces, 230 yards

(113 grams, 183 meters) per skein]:

Hat

☐ 1 skein

Scarf

☐ 2 skeins

Crochet Hook

☐ Size H (5 mm)

or size needed for gauge

Additional Supplies

☐ Yarn needle

GAUGE INFORMATION

In pattern,

15 sts and 12 rows = 4" (10 cm)

Gauge Swatch: 5¼"w x 3"h

(13.25 cm x 7.5 cm)

Work same as Hat Band for 9 rows; do **not** finish off.

STITCH GUIDE

FRONT POST TREBLE CROCHET ***(abbreviated FPtr)***

YO twice, insert hook from **front** to **back** around post of st indicated ***(Fig. 4, page 30)***, YO and pull up a loop (4 loops on hook), (YO and draw through 2 loops on hook) 3 times.

FRONT POST DOUBLE TREBLE CROCHET ***(abbreviated FPdtr)***

YO 3 times, insert hook from **front** to **back** around post of st indicated ***(Fig. 4, page 30)***, YO and pull up a loop (5 loops on hook), (YO and draw through 2 loops on hook) 4 times.

HALF DOUBLE 2 TOGETHER ***(abbreviated hdc2tog)*** (uses next 2 sts)

★ YO, insert hook in **next** hdc, YO and pull up a loop; repeat from ★ once **more**, YO and draw through all 5 loops on hook (**counts as one hdc**).

HAT

BAND

Row 1 (Right side)**:** Hdc in back ridge of third ch from hook ***(Fig. 1, page 30)*** **(2 skipped chs count as first hdc, now and throughout)** and each ch across: 21 hdc.

Row 2: Ch 2 (**counts as first hdc, now and throughout**), turn; hdc in next hdc and in each hdc across.

Row 3: Ch 2, turn; hdc in next hdc, ★ † skip next 3 hdc, work FPdtr around each hdc one row **below** next 2 hdc, skip 2 hdc from last hdc made, hdc in next hdc, working in **front** of last 2 FPdtr made, work FPdtr around each hdc one row **below** 2 skipped hdc (Cable made), skip next 2 hdc from last hdc made †, hdc in next hdc; repeat from ★ once **more**, then repeat from † to † once, hdc in last 2 hdc: 12 FPdtr and 9 hdc.

Row 4 AND ALL WRONG SIDE ROWS: Ch 2, turn; hdc in next hdc and in each st across.

Row 5: Ch 2, turn; hdc in next hdc, work FPtr around each of next 2 FPdtr one row **below**, skip next 2 hdc from last hdc made, hdc in next hdc, ★ skip next 2 FPdtr one row **below**, work FPdtr around each of next 2 FPdtr, skip next 2 hdc from last hdc made, hdc in next hdc, working **behind** last 2 FPdtr made, work FPdtr around each of 2 skipped FPdtr **(Cable made)**, skip next 2 hdc from last hdc made, hdc in next hdc; repeat from ★ once **more**, work FPtr around each of next 2 FPdtr one row **below**, skip next 2 hdc from last hdc made, hdc in last 2 hdc: 8 FPdtr, 4 FPtr, and 9 hdc.

Row 7: Ch 2, turn; hdc in next hdc, ★ † skip next 2 FPsts one row **below**, work FPdtr around each of next 2 FPsts, skip next 2 hdc from last hdc made, hdc in next hdc, working in **front** of last 2 FPdtr made, work FPdtr around each of 2 skipped FPsts **(Cable made)**, skip next 2 hdc from last hdc made †, hdc in next hdc; repeat from ★ once **more**, then repeat from † to † once, hdc in last 2 hdc: 12 FPdtr and 9 hdc.

Row 9: Ch 2, turn; hdc in next hdc, work FPtr around each of next 2 FPdtr one row **below**, skip next 2 hdc from last hdc made, hdc in next hdc, ★ skip next 2 FPdtr one row **below**, work FPdtr around each of next 2 FPdtr, skip next 2 hdc from last hdc made, hdc in next hdc, working **behind** last 2 FPdtr made, work FPdtr around each of 2 skipped FPdtr **(Cable made)**, skip next 2 hdc from last hdc made, hdc in next hdc; repeat from ★ once **more**, work FPtr around each of next 2 FPdtr one row **below**, skip next 2 hdc from last hdc made, hdc in last 2 hdc: 8 FPdtr, 4 FPtr, and 9 hdc.

Repeat Rows 6-9 for pattern until Band measures approximately 21" (53.5 cm) from beginning ch, ending by working Row 8.

Finish off leaving a long end for sewing.

With **wrong** side together, fold Band in half with last row and beginning ch edge together. Whipstitch stitches together to form a ring *(Fig. 7a, page 31)*.

SHAPING

Rnd 1: With **right** side facing, join yarn with hdc at seam *(see Joining With Hdc, page 30)*; work 76 hdc evenly spaced around ends of rows; join with slip st to first hdc: 77 hdc.

Rnd 2: Ch 2, hdc in next 8 hdc, hdc2tog, (hdc in next 9 hdc, hdc2tog) around; join with slip st to first hdc: 70 hdc.

Rnd 3: Ch 2, hdc in next 7 hdc, hdc2tog, (hdc in next 8 hdc, hdc2tog) around; join with slip st to first hdc: 63 hdc.

Rnd 4: Ch 2, hdc in next 6 hdc, hdc2tog, (hdc in next 7 hdc, hdc2tog) around; join with slip st to first hdc: 56 hdc.

Rnd 5: Ch 2, hdc in next hdc, hdc2tog, (hdc in next 2 hdc, hdc2tog) around; join with slip st to first hdc: 42 hdc.

Rnd 6: Ch 2, hdc2tog, (hdc in next hdc, hdc2tog) around; join with slip st to first hdc: 28 hdc.

Rnds 7 and 8: Ch 1, skip first st, hdc in next hdc, hdc2tog around; join with slip st to first hdc: 7 hdc.

Finish off leaving a long end for sewing.

Thread yarn needle with long end and weave needle through remaining hdc on Rnd 8 *(Fig. A, page 19)*; gather **tightly** to close and secure end.

SCARF

Ch 34.

Row 1 (Right side)**:** Hdc in back ridge of third ch from hook and each ch across: 33 hdc.

Row 2 AND ALL WRONG SIDE ROWS: Ch 2, turn; hdc in next hdc and in each st across.

Row 3: Ch 2, turn; hdc in next hdc, ★ † skip next 3 hdc, work FPdtr around each hdc one row **below** next 2 hdc, skip 2 hdc from last hdc made, hdc in next hdc, working in **front** of last 2 FPdtr made, work FPdtr around each hdc one row **below** 2 skipped hdc (**Cable made**), skip next 2 hdc from last hdc made †, hdc in next hdc; repeat from ★ 3 times **more**, then repeat from † to † once, hdc in last 2 hdc: 20 FPdtr and 13 hdc.

Row 5: Ch 2, turn; hdc in next hdc, work FPtr around each of next 2 FPdtr one row **below**, skip next 2 hdc from last hdc made, hdc in next hdc, ★ skip next 2 FPdtr one row **below**, work FPdtr around each of next 2 FPdtr, skip next 2 hdc from last hdc made, hdc in next hdc, working **behind** last 2 FPdtr made, work FPdtr around each of 2 skipped FPdtr (**Cable made**), skip next 2 hdc from last hdc made, hdc in next hdc; repeat from ★ 3 times **more**, work FPtr around each of next 2 FPdtr one row **below**, skip next 2 hdc from last hdc made, hdc in last 2 hdc: 16 FPdtr, 4 FPtr, and 13 hdc.

Row 7: Ch 2, turn; hdc in next hdc, ★ † skip next 2 FPsts one row **below**, work FPdtr around each of next 2 FPsts, skip next 2 hdc from last hdc made, hdc in next hdc, working in **front** of last 2 FPdtr made, work FPdtr around each of 2 skipped FPsts (**Cable made**), skip next 2 hdc from last hdc made †, hdc in next hdc; repeat from ★ 3 times **more**, then repeat from † to † once, hdc in last 2 hdc: 20 FPdtr and 13 hdc.

Row 9: Ch 2, turn; hdc in next hdc, work FPtr around each of next 2 FPdtr one row **below**, skip next 2 hdc from last hdc made, hdc in next hdc, ★ skip next 2 FPdtr one row **below**, work FPdtr around each of next 2 FPdtr, skip next 2 hdc from last hdc made, hdc in next hdc, working **behind** last 2 FPdtr made, work FPdtr around each of 2 skipped FPdtr (**Cable made**), skip next 2 hdc from last hdc made, hdc in next hdc; repeat from ★ 3 times **more**, work FPtr around each of next 2 FPdtr one row **below**, skip next 2 hdc from last hdc made, hdc in last 2 hdc: 16 FPdtr, 4 FPtr, and 13 hdc.

Repeat Rows 6-9 for pattern until Scarf measures approximately 54" (137 cm) from beginning ch, ending by working Row 8.

Last Row: Ch 2, turn; hdc in next hdc and in each st across; finish off.

Designs by Melissa Leapman.

(Additional Color Option)

Car Seat Blanket

●●○○ EASY **Finished Size:** 22" wide x 29¾" high (56.5 cm x 75.5 cm)

SHOPPING LIST

Yarn (Medium Weight) 4 MEDIUM

[5 ounces, 251 yards (142 grams, 230 meters) per skein]:

☐ 3 skeins

Crochet Hook

☐ Size J (6 mm)

or size needed for gauge

GAUGE INFORMATION

16 dc = 5¾" (14.5 cm);
10 rows = 6¾"(17.25 cm)

Gauge Swatch: 5¾" wide x 6¾" high (14.5 cm x 17.25 cm)

Ch 18.

Row 1: Working in back ridges of beginning ch *(Fig. 1, page 30)*, dc in fourth ch from hook **(3 skipped chs count as first dc)** and in each ch across: 16 dc.

Rows 2-10: Ch 3 **(counts as first dc)**, turn; dc in next dc and in each dc across.

Finish off.

STITCH GUIDE

CROSS ST (uses next 2 dc)

Skip next dc, dc in next dc, working **behind** last dc made, dc in skipped dc.

BLANKET

Ch 64.

Row 1 (Wrong side)**:** Working in back ridge of beginning ch *(Fig. 1, page 30)*, dc in fourth ch from hook **(3 skipped chs count as first dc)** and in each ch across: 62 dc.

Rows 2 and 3: Ch 3 **(counts as first dc, now and throughout)**, turn; dc in next dc and in each dc across.

Rows 4-41: Ch 3, turn; dc in next 4 dc, work 26 Cross Sts, dc in last 4 dc.

Rows 42-44: Ch 3, turn; dc in next dc and in each dc across.

Finish off.

Design by Becky Stevens.

(Additional Color Option)

Chevron Accent Bag

●●○○ EASY **Finished Size:** 9½" wide x 9" high (24 cm x 23 cm) excluding Handle

SHOPPING LIST

Yarn (Medium Weight) 4 MEDIUM

[5 ounces, 256 yards
(141 grams, 234 meters) per skein]:

- ☐ Grey - 1 skein

[4 ounces, 204 yards
(113 grams, 187 meters) per skein]:

- ☐ Variegated - 1 skein

Crochet Hook

- ☐ Size H (5 mm)
  or size needed for gauge

Additional Supplies

- ☐ Yarn needle

GAUGE INFORMATION

14 dc and 8 rows = 4" (10 cm)

Gauge Swatch: 4" (10 cm) square

With Grey, ch 16.

Row 1: Dc in fourth ch from hook (**3 skipped chs count as first dc**) and in each ch across: 14 dc.

Rows 2-8: Ch 3 (**counts as first dc**), turn; dc in next dc and in each dc across.

Finish off.

BODY (Make 2)

With Grey, ch 36, place marker in fourth ch from hook for Handle placement.

Row 1 (Right side)**:** Working in back ridge of beginning ch ***(Fig. 1, page 30)***, sc in second ch from hook and in next 16 chs, 3 sc in next ch, sc in each ch across: 37 sc.

Note: Loop a short piece of yarn around any stitch to mark Row 1 as **right** side.

Row 2: Ch 2 (**does not count as a st, now and throughout**), turn; dc in first sc, skip next sc, dc in next 16 sc, 3 dc in next sc, dc in next 16 sc, skip next sc, dc in last sc.

Rows 3-17: Ch 2, turn; dc in first dc, skip next dc, dc in next 16 dc, 3 dc in next dc, dc in next dc and in each dc across to last 2 dc, skip next dc, dc in last dc.

Finish off.

CENTER CHEVRON

With Variegated, ch 14.

Row 1 (Right side)**:** Working in back ridge of beginning ch, sc in second ch from hook and in next 5 chs, 3 sc in next ch, sc in each ch across: 15 sc.

Note: Mark Row 1 as **right** side.

Row 2: Ch 3 (**counts as first dc, now and throughout**), turn; skip next sc, dc in next 5 sc, 3 dc in next sc, dc in next 5 sc, skip next sc, dc in last sc.

Rows 3-17: Ch 3, turn; skip next dc, dc in next 5 dc, 3 dc in next dc, dc in next 5 sc, skip next dc, dc in last dc.

Finish off leaving a long end for sewing.

Place **wrong** side of Center Chevron on center **right** side of one Body, matching beginning chs. Using long end, sew Center Chevron in place.

With **wrong** sides together, sew Body side and bottom seams.

HANDLE

Row 1: With **right** side facing and working in free loops of beginning ch ***(Fig. 3, page 30)***, join Grey with sc in marked ch ***(see Joining With Sc, page 30)***; sc in next 5 chs: 6 sc.

Rows 2-60: Ch 1, turn; sc in each sc across.

Finish off leaving a long end for sewing.

Beginning in marked ch on opposite side of Bag, sew Handle to Bag.

Design by Kristi Simpson.

General Instructions

ABBREVIATIONS

ch(s)	chain(s)
cm	centimeters
dc	double crochet(s)
dtr	double treble crochet(s)
FPdtr	Front Post double treble crochet(s)
FPtr	Front Post treble crochet(s)
FPst	Front Post stitch(es)
hdc	half double crochet(s)
hdc2tog	half double crochet 2 together
mm	millimeters
Rnd(s)	Round(s)
sc	single crochet(s)
sc2tog	single crochet 2 together
sp(s)	space(s)
st(s)	stitch(es)
tr	treble crochet(s)
YO	yarn over

CROCHET TERMINOLOGY		
UNITED STATES		INTERNATIONAL
slip stitch (slip st)	=	single crochet (sc)
single crochet (sc)	=	double crochet (dc)
half double crochet (hdc)	=	half treble crochet (htr)
double crochet (dc)	=	treble crochet (tr)
treble crochet (tr)	=	double treble crochet (dtr)
double treble crochet (dtr)	=	triple treble crochet (ttr)
triple treble crochet (tr tr)	=	quadruple treble crochet (qtr)
skip	=	miss

SYMBOLS & TERMS

★ — work instructions following ★ as many **more** times as indicated in addition to the first time.

† to † — work all instructions from first † to second † **as many** times as specified.

( ) or **[ ]** — work enclosed instructions **as many** times as specified by the number immediately following **or** work all enclosed instructions in the stitch or space indicated **or** contains explanatory remarks.

colon (:) — the number(s) given after a colon at the end of a row or round denote(s) the number of stitches or spaces you should have on that row or round.

GAUGE

Exact gauge is **essential** for proper size. Before beginning your project, make the sample swatch given in the individual instructions in the yarn and hook specified. After completing the swatch, measure it, counting your stitches and rows/rounds carefully. If your swatch is larger or smaller than specified, **make another, changing hook size to get the correct gauge**. Keep trying until you find the size hook that will give you the specified gauge.

MARKERS

Markers are used to help distinguish the beginning of each round being worked. Place a 2" (5 cm) scrap piece of yarn before the first stitch of each round, moving marker after each round is complete.

●○○○ **BEGINNER**	Projects for first-time crocheters using basic stitches. Minimal shaping.
●●○○ **EASY**	Projects using yarn with basic stitches, repetitive stitch patterns, simple color changes, and simple shaping and finishing.
●●●○ **INTERMEDIATE**	Projects using a variety of techniques, such as basic lace patterns or color patterns, mid-level shaping and finishing.
●●●● **EXPERIENCED**	Projects with intricate stitch patterns, techniques and dimension, such as non-repeating patterns, multi-color techniques, fine threads, small hooks, detailed shaping and refined finishing.

CROCHET HOOKS

U.S.	B-1	C-2	D-3	E-4	F-5	G-6	7	H-8	I-9	J-10	K-10½	L-11	M/N-13	N/P-15	P/Q	Q	S
Metric - mm	2.25	2.75	3.25	3.5	3.75	4	4.5	5	5.5	6	6.5	8	9	10	15	16	19

JOINING WITH SC

When instructed to join with sc, begin with a slip knot on hook. Insert hook in stitch or space indicated, YO and pull up a loop, YO and draw through both loops on hook.

JOINING WITH HDC

When instructed to join with hdc, begin with a slip knot on hook. YO, holding loop on hook, insert hook in stitch or space indicated, YO and pull up a loop (3 loops on hook), YO and draw through all 3 loops on hook.

BACK RIDGE

Work only in loops indicated by arrows ***(Fig. 1)***.

Fig. 1

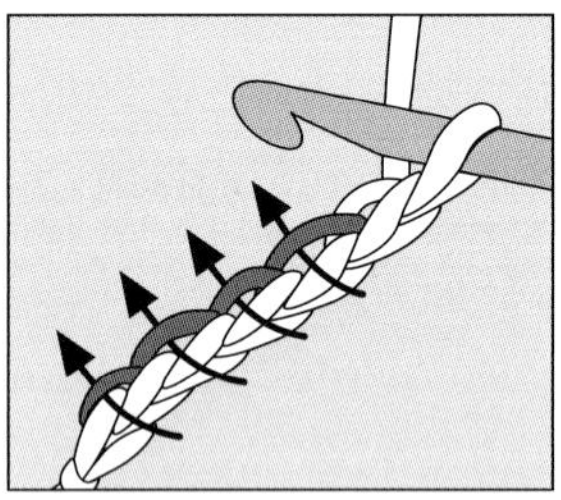

BACK LOOP ONLY

Work only in loop(s) indicated by arrow ***(Fig. 2)***.

Fig. 2

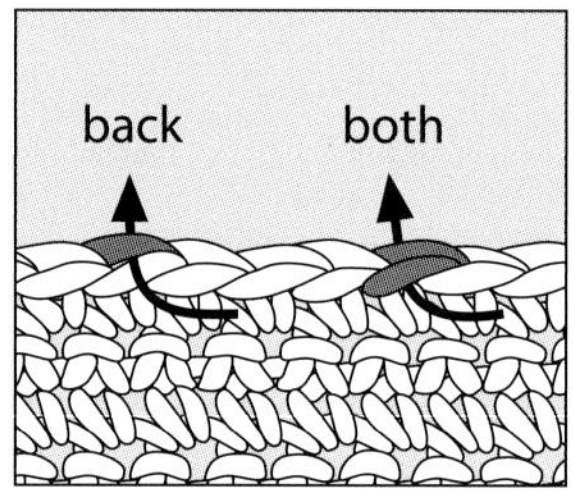

FREE LOOPS OF A CHAIN

When instructed to work in free loops of a chain, work in loop indicated by arrow ***(Fig. 3)***.

Fig. 3

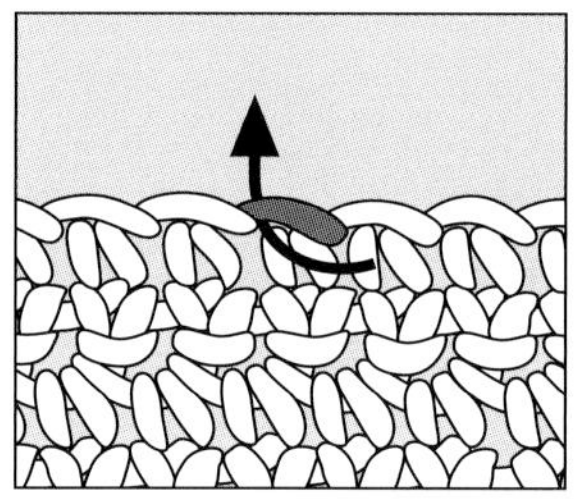

POST STITCH

Work around post of stitch indicated, inserting hook in direction of arrow ***(Fig. 4)***.

Fig. 4

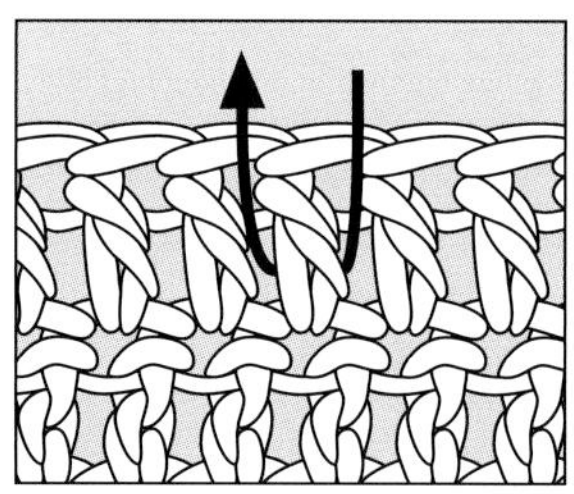

CHANGING COLORS

YO, insert hook in stitch indicated, YO and pull up a loop, YO and draw through 2 loops on hook, drop yarn, with new yarn ***(Fig. 5)***, YO and draw through 2 loops on hook.

Fig. 5

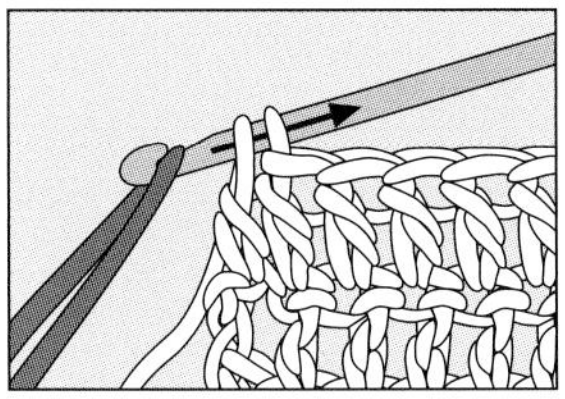

WORKING IN SPACE BEFORE A STITCH

When instructed to work in space **before** a stitch or in spaces **between** stitches, insert hook in space indicated by arrow ***(Fig. 6)***.

Fig. 6

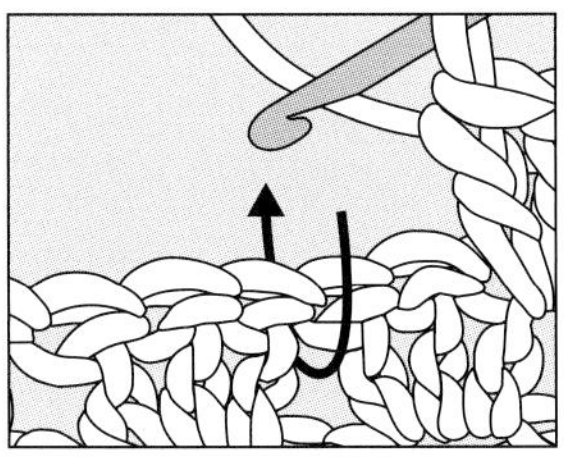

WHIPSTITCH

With **wrong** sides together, sew through both pieces once to secure the beginning of the seam, leaving an ample yarn end to weave in later. Insert the needle from **back** to **front** through **both** loops of each stitch on **both** pieces ***(Fig. 7a)*** **or** in ends of rows ***(Fig. 7b)***. Bring the needle around and insert it from **back** to **front** through the next stitch or strands on both pieces.
Repeat, being careful to match stitches and rows.

Fig. 7a

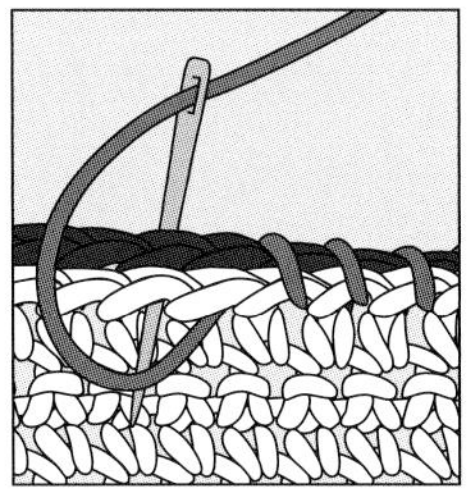

Fig. 7b

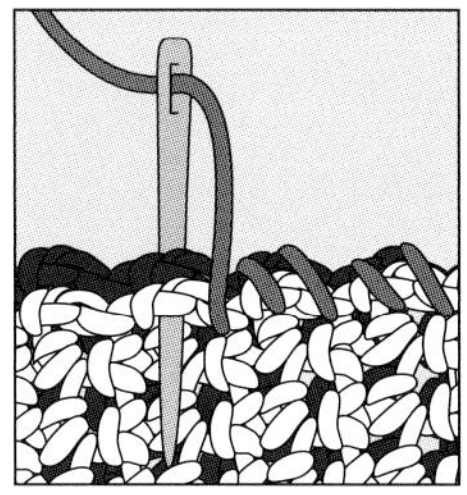

Yarn Weight Symbol & Names	LACE 0	SUPER FINE 1	FINE 2	LIGHT 3	MEDIUM 4	BULKY 5	SUPER BULKY 6	JUMBO 7
Type of Yarns in Category	Fingering, size 10 crochet thread	Sock, Fingering, Baby	Sport, Baby	DK, Light Worsted	Worsted, Afghan, Aran	Chunky, Craft, Rug	Super Bulky, Roving	Jumbo, Roving
Crochet Gauge* Ranges in Single Crochet to 4" (10 cm)	32-42 sts**	21-32 sts	16-20 sts	12-17 sts	11-14 sts	8-11 sts	6-9 sts	5 sts and fewer
Advised Hook Size Range	Steel*** 6 to 8, Regular hook B-1	B-1 to E-4	E-4 to 7	7 to I-9	I-9 to K-10½	K-10½ to M/N-13	M/N-13 to Q	Q and larger

*GUIDELINES ONLY: The chart above reflects the most commonly used gauges and hook sizes for specific yarn categories.

** Lace weight yarns are usually crocheted with larger hooks to create lacy openwork patterns. Accordingly, a gauge range is difficult to determine. Always follow the gauge stated in your pattern.

*** Steel crochet hooks are sized differently from regular hooks–the higher the number, the smaller the hook, which is the reverse of regular hook sizing.

Yarn Information

The items in this book were made using a variety of yarn weights. Any brand of the specific weight of yarn may be used. It is best to refer to the yardage/meters when determining how many balls or skeins to purchase. Remember, to achieve the same look, it is the weight of yarn that is important, not the brand of yarn.

For your convenience, listed below are the specific yarns used to create our photography models. Because yarn manufacturers make frequent changes to their product lines, you may sometimes find it necessary to use a substitute yarn or to search for the discontinued product at alternate suppliers (locally or online).

CABLED AFGHAN
Red Heart® Grande™
#0934 Winter Lake

RIPPLE AFGHAN
Caron® Simply Soft®
Dk Grey - #9508 Charcoal Heather
Lt Grey - #9509 Grey Heather
Yellow - #9773 Neon Yellow

RUG
Red Heart® Strata™
#2405 Grey

PLUSH PILLOW
Red Heart® Soft®
#9440 Light Grey Heather

CUP COZY
Lion Brand® Vanna's Choice®
#500 Patchwork Grey

ZIGZAG DISHCLOTH
Premier® Home® Cotton
Grey - #44-20 Grey Splash
White - #38-01 White

TRENDSETTER HAT
Lion Brand® Vanna's Choice®
Grey - #149 Silver Grey
Red - #180 Cranberry

SEXTON BRAID HAT & SCARF
Lion Brand® Heartland®
#350 Mount Rainier Tweed
Color Option -
Caron® Simply Soft®
#0008 Autumn Maize

CAR SEAT BLANKET
Lion Brand® Heartland®
#151 Katmai
Color Option -
Bernat® Giggles™
#56230 Giggling Green

CHEVRON ACCENT BAG
Red Heart® Soft®
Grey - #9010 Charcoal
Variegated - #9931 Greyscale

We have made every effort to ensure that these instructions are accurate and complete. We cannot, however, be responsible for human error, typographical mistakes, or variations in individual work.

Items made and instructions tested by Janet Akins and Raymelle Greening.

Production Team: Instructional/ Technical Editor - Sarah J. Green; Editorial Writer - Sarah Green; Senior Graphic Artist - Lora Puls; Graphic Artist - Kytanna McFarlin; Photo Stylist - Lori Wenger; and Photographer - Ken West.